the language of shalom

7 keys to practical reconciliation

Cheryl Miller

with foreword by John M. Perkins

QUANTUM CIRCLES PRESS

Victoria, Texas

ISBN 978-0-9859546-0-4

Scriptures labeled NIV are taken from THE HOLY BIBLE, NEW INTERNATIONAL VERSION®, NIV® Copyright © 1973, 1978, 1984, 2011 by Biblica, Inc.™ Used by permission. All rights reserved worldwide.

Scriptures labeled NIV1984 are taken from the HOLY BIBLE, NEW INTERNATIONAL VERSION®. Copyright © 1973, 1978, 1984 Biblica. Used by permission of Zondervan. All rights reserved.

Scriptures labeled NKJV are taken from the New King James Version. Copyright © 1982 by Thomas Nelson, Inc. Used by permission. All rights reserved.

Scriptures labeled NLV are taken from the New Life Version. Copyright © 1969 by Christian Literature International. Used by permission. All rights reserved.

Scriptures labeled KJV are taken from THE HOLY BIBLE, KING JAMES VERSION, 1611.

Photo of Cheryl Miller by Kevin Jordan © 2012

*This book is dedicated to Beverly and James,
whom God used to transform my future
and the future of my children.
You will always be my heroes.*

contents

foreword

When I met Cheryl Miller several years ago and heard of her background and experience, I encouraged her to think about writing a book to help others understand the concepts she had implemented in her work in Victoria, Texas. Cheryl's work as a restorative justice mediator gives her unique insight into speaking in a way that facilitates peace. Cheryl also runs a community development ministry that has been successful in creating an environment where the women she works with have the opportunity for significant life transformation. Bringing the principles of restorative justice and mediation into the field of Christian community development (CCD), the processes in this book not only complement the components of CCD work but can actually take the components to new levels of effectiveness. I was glad to see that she has taken up that challenge in this book.

Many problems of our urban communities stem from individuals' doubts about their self-worth. They don't see the inherent dignity that God has instilled in each one of us. So my job as a Christian community developer, in large part, is to speak into these broken spirits, to tell them, "You are beautiful the way you are." We are often dealing with people who simply can't accept this statement, so we try to affirm this dignity, this beauty, this sense of worth in them. We say, "I truly see it; I just need to help you see it as well."

Over the past few years I have noticed that young people today are viewing race differently. Oftentimes it seems they don't even notice if someone is of a different nationality. The issues that have historically been barriers to the human race are hindering this generation less and less, and I see this generation emerging as one that looks at nationality and ethnicity in a more affirming way. They can affirm differences as healthy parts of the mix. They don't see people as needing to be fixed.

Watching this younger generation grow into people who take other people for who they are has caused me to realize that we cannot keep talking about reconciliation, race, and community using language of the past. There is a need for a new language, a new way to express our goals, our hopes, and our dreams of a better community. *The Language of Shalom* begins this conversation about developing a new language. This book provides tools and means to communicate in a new way that can allow us to build and reconcile relationships and strengthen communities. Its concepts and processes can help us become peacemakers by learning to harness the power of the spoken word.

I believe this book is beneficial to us as individuals, as community development workers, as neighbors, and as Christians seeking to live out the call to get started as ministers of reconciliation. This upcoming generation can benefit from learning to speak the language of shalom. Those who have walked this journey need to follow suit and begin learning this language as well. From my years of working with people, I believe these processes can be a new beginning to the way we speak and seek to build shalom.

—John M. Perkins

Co-founder and chairman, Christian
Community Development Association

President, John M. Perkins Foundation for
Reconciliation and Development

my story

…But where sin abounded, grace did much more abound…

—Romans 5:20 KJV

In May 1987 I was a single pregnant woman. I had been working in a bar in Fort Worth before finding out I was pregnant,
and I continued to work there until it was no longer an option.
Once my income was gone, even the ratty, one-bedroom duplex
in a bad neighborhood was more than I could maintain.

I had made many bad choices over the previous ten years,
and starting over was costly. Fortunately my sister and her
husband took on the financial and emotional burden of bringing me home to live with them and their three young daughters.
They supported me, but they also expected me to work hard and
to make changes. In July, two months after Beverly took me in,
I went into labor—ten weeks early. It was then that I discovered
I was having twins! Because of the risk, I was taken by ambu-
lance to a different hospital than I had planned for delivery. The

babies only weighed three pounds each and had numerous health problems. So my first two children were born to a welfare mother whom many would have called a hopeless case.

My own journey, however, has shown me that nobody is hopeless. Anybody can change with God's help. In my case, God used my sister to love, guide, and help me that year. Many people would have felt sorry for me and allowed me to feel sorry for myself, but not my sister. She insisted that I return to college and finish my teaching degree. Her model of love, coupled with her expectation that I take responsibility for my life, became the model that I use with women at the Perpetual Help Home where I now work. But I'm getting ahead of myself.

In the summer of 1987 I had a lot of challenges. I had no money and twins who were very sick and required a great deal of care. Beverly helped me with the children while I commuted forty-five minutes each way to school and then back to work. It was a strenuous time for me, but I learned that I was going to have to work hard to change my future and the future of my children. Within a few months I was making enough money from my Pell Grant and the salary from my new job to move out of Bev's house and closer to school. Almost two years after I went to live with her, I finished my education degree. The next day I married my husband, Leslie, whom I had met at the country-western bar where I had begun working after I had the twins. Although I was making headway, I still had many issues that God needed to bring me out of.

After graduation, Leslie and I settled down, and I began teaching elementary school. Although I had changed in many ways, I was still struggling and making bad choices. The last time I used drugs was during the summer of 1988. One weekend I used meth and cocaine in significant amounts. I thought I might be pregnant but wasn't sure, so I just dismissed the thought. After returning from that party weekend, I found out that I was about six weeks pregnant with our son, Trey. I never used drugs again.

The following year I had a classroom of children who were struggling with major issues, which made me question why God had allowed these things to happen. I wanted to help them and was trying to figure out how I could do that. Once again, Beverly suggested that I ask God for wisdom and then trust Him. I got down on my knees in my bedroom and told God that I needed His wisdom. Not only that, but I told Him that I was ready to lay everything down and trust Him with my life. Shortly after that, two men knocked on my door and invited me to Northside Baptist Church. I went, made a profession of faith, and was baptized. I have gone to Northside ever since. My whole family followed suit, including Leslie.

In 1996, after seven years of teaching, I began to feel that God wanted me to do something else. So I quit teaching and decided to figure out my new path. The first thing that happened was that God brought our oldest child, Jamie, into our family. Jamie had been a student of mine several years earlier. When we found out that she had no place to go, we took her into our home, and she has been our daughter ever since. This was the beginning of God's allowing me to love someone else as He has loved me.

In July 1999, I went to volunteer at a local ministry called Perpetual Help Home and found out that the director was resigning. Three days later I began working as the executive director of Perpetual Help Home. At that time the ministry was just a small housing program for women who had been incarcerated, operating in a seven-bedroom facility. Over the course of the last thirteen years, we have grown to fifty bedrooms in two communities. We offer various programs and assist women in any crisis situation.

During the first six months of working at Perpetual Help Home, I heard about a program that utilized victim-offender mediation (VOM) to help victims of crime meet with the offenders who had committed the crimes against them. Many times this process helps crime victims heal. I had taken mediation training when I was a teacher, so I was intrigued with the idea. We were doing so much for the ex-offenders at Perpetual Help, but could we help the victims as well? I felt it was important to address crime from both sides of the issue, so I signed up for the training. Soon I completed the VOM training and eventually became a Credentialed Advanced Mediator. I have volunteered as a mediator between victims of crime and offenders in Texas for the last thirteen years.

As I facilitated mediations for some of the most extreme crimes, I witnessed the amazing healing and reconciliation power of the mediation process. I started trying to figure out ways to incorporate these restorative justice principles into our Perpetual Help programs. Little by little, we have worked to infuse these concepts into all aspects of Perpetual Help Home and our other related ministries.

As I learned more about restorative justice principles, I realized that I needed to live by those principles as well. A topic we discuss with women at Perpetual Help Home is accountability for harm, and one evening it hit me that I had never been accountable for my past harms. When our youngest son, Trey, was sixteen, I confessed that I had used drugs when I was pregnant with him. Deeply ashamed, I admitted to him all my selfish choices that could have damaged his future. Sobbing under the weight of that shame, I asked him to forgive me for my selfishness. He left his seat and came over and embraced me. "Of course I forgive you," he said. It was as if God had witnessed my sin and the damage that could have been done sixteen years before and said, "Not this child. I will protect him in his mother's womb." As a sign, Trey tattooed Romans 5:20 on his wrist: "But where sin abounded, grace did much more abound."

In May 2002, I received a master's degree in nonprofit leadership and communication. As I walked through the halls of the university during my last week on campus, I kept thinking, "Fifteen years ago, I was single, pregnant, and on welfare. How did I get here?" My whole life is proof that where sin abounded, God's grace abounded more.

Sometimes I sit on the swing in my backyard and ask God why He has blessed me so. I was wicked and lost, yet He saw fit not only to rescue me but to bless me abundantly. My children are all doing well. Dani, one of the premature twins, is on full scholarship, seeking Master of Divinity and Master of Social Work dual degrees from Truett Seminary and Baylor University. She was a softball player in college and helped coach the team to an NCAA National Championship after her graduation. Her twin brother, Travis, graduated from the United States Air Force Academy and is a first lieutenant in pilot training. Trey was a national champion debater in college and just graduated from East Texas Baptist University; he is now in full-time ministry. Jamie has graduated from college and is pursuing her dream of raising a family and working with children. I can say that my life is truly a reflection of the scripture in Romans 5:20: I had sin and sin abundant, but indeed grace has abundantly abounded beyond my wildest dreams.

I know there is no way I can repay my sister and her husband for the gift of grace they gave me. I guess I can only live my life in a way that says *Thank You!* to them and God for that gift. Sharing these concepts with you is one way for me to do that.

shalom.

Therefore, if anyone is in Christ, he is a new creation; old things have passed away; behold, all things have become new. Now all things are of God, who has reconciled us to Himself through Jesus Christ, and has given us the ministry of reconciliation...
—2 Corinthians 5:17-18 NKJV

I have written this book to offer some simple steps in facilitating reconciliation. My hope is to help Christian community developers and just plain folks learn basic concepts and processes of restorative justice. This book only scratches the surface of everything we can do to become better ministers of reconciliation. I hope reading this whets your appetite to learn more, seek more, and study more. My prayer is that this guide will help you become a reconciler who brings the gospel of peace and healing to broken relationships in your family, community, and ministry.

My experience in working as a mediator and a director of a community-based ministry has led me to believe that the fields of restorative justice and Christian community development should be brought together. Mediation skills and processes are the threads that weave these two practices together. When Christian community development, restorative justice, and mediation merge, they create a new type of communication called the *language of shalom*. This language is all about justice, wholeness, soundness, well-being, peace, and reconciliation.

I have watched victims and offenders come to mediation apprehensive, only to leave, a few hours later, empowered, with a dramatically changed view of themselves, of the crime, or of life. Somewhere along the way of volunteering as a mediator, I became a reconciler and began to view the world through the eyes of a reconciler. When that happened, I began to see reconciliation opportunities everywhere. I realized that standard means of communication are incapable of facilitating reconciliation in such profound ways.

There should be two goals of reconciliation among people. The first is *justice*, where things are made right. Mediation is a proven model for facilitating justice. The second goal should be *shalom,* which means "well-being in general; all good in relation to both man and God."

Injustice, or conflict, can be seen as an iceberg. It is easy to see evidence of injustice jutting forth, requiring some form of corrective action. But it is vital to realize that there are currents that run deep beneath what we see on the surface. The language of shalom is the tool that can be used to address what is beneath the surface.

The language of shalom encompasses more than the simpler term *mediation*. A reconciler speaking the language of shalom seeks reconciliation but goes even further to help make friends of enemies.

This new language is more appropriate to describe reconciliation in a ministry context because it places conflict and reconciliation where they should rightly be: in the shadow of Christ. He knows those deep places in our hearts and reaches out to bring healing. Christ is the perfect fullness of both mediator and reconciler.

By studying the following chapters, you can learn the language of shalom and start on the road to becoming a more effective Christian community developer and minister of reconciliation. Each chapter concludes with opportunities to take things further. These questions and ideas will help you find practical ways to start becoming a dynamic minister of reconciliation or to take your skills to the next level.

the language of shalom.

**Study Restorative Justice
& Basic Mediation**

*Finally, brothers and sisters, rejoice! Strive for full **restoration**, encourage one another, be of one mind, live in peace. And the God of love and peace will be with you.*

—2 Corinthians 13:11 NIV

W orking concepts of restorative justice into our lives is challenging and exciting. God calls us to a lifestyle of reconciliation. Christ alluded to the concept of reconciliation in Matthew 5:43-47 NIV 1984:

"You have heard that it was said, 'Love your neighbor and hate your enemy.' But I tell you: Love your enemies and pray for those who persecute you, that you may be sons of your Father in heaven. He causes his sun to rise on the evil and the good, and sends rain on the righteous and the unrighteous. If you love those who love you, what reward will you get? Are not even the tax collectors doing that? And if you greet only your brothers, what are you doing more than others? Do not even pagans do that?"

This scripture is a cornerstone on which reconciliation can be built. If someone is an enemy, he or she must have hurt or offended us somehow. Harm must have taken place. Sometimes we might consider an individual or group who is opposed to our goals as an enemy. In Matthew 5, Christ challenges us to love our enemies. He does not give us permission to avoid or ignore those who are opposed to us or who have harmed us. Nor does He give us permission to deal with them in anger. He merely issues His command: *Love.*

In the United States we have a retributive justice system. This means that our society's position as reflected in our laws is that punishment, when proportionally appropriate, is an acceptable response to crime and injustice. Restorative justice, however, approaches crime in a more holistic way. There is acknowledgment that laws have been broken, but there is also the understanding that harm has been done to individuals. Restorative justice recognizes that harm and seeks to restore and repair individuals on a physical, spiritual, and emotional level.

Ron Claassen of Fresno Pacific University collaborated with the county of Fresno, California, to produce *Restorative Justice: A Framework for Fresno.* He defines the concept in this way: "Restorative Justice is a way of responding to conflict, misbehavior, and crime that makes things as right as possible for all who were impacted. Restorative justice includes recognizing the conflict or harm, repairing the damage (physical and relational) as much as possible, and creating future accountability plans and/or agreements that will prevent the same thing from happening again. Restorative justice includes programs, processes, and procedures that are guided by Restorative Justice Principles"

Restorative justice reinforces the Christian community development concept of relocation in that it recognizes that outsiders can never understand all the dynamics of community issues. Community members may easily determine all who are involved in or affected by an issue, but there are also times when it is necessary to find an individual slightly removed from the conflict or injustice to facilitate a dialogue that can bring reconciliation. This can be someone in the neighborhood not directly involved in a conflict. But when the conflict or injustice involves the entire community, it may become necessary to seek an outside, neutral facilitator.

There are a variety of community-based restorative justice models emerging as alternatives to traditional law enforcement processes—victim-offender dialogue, restorative circles, family group conferences, community restorative boards, sentencing circles, and support circles, to name a few. These processes work effectively in situations that involve a crime against an individual in a community. However, they can also be helpful in many other conflicts. They do require more training than will be addressed in this book, but the names are included to provide a launch pad for further study. What most of these processes have in common is that they identify everyone involved in a conflict and bring them together to determine the most effective resolution to a problem.

Identify Stakeholders

A stakeholder is one who is involved in or affected by a course of action. Restorative justice requires that all stakeholders be part of reconciliation by having a voice in the process. Identifying all the stakeholders in a given situation or problem is necessary for reconciliation. Please note that it is rare that a problem involves only two individuals. There may be a primary point of conflict between two individuals, but more often than not, there are other people who must also be included to facilitate a complete reconciliation. When all the stakeholders are involved, there is a greater chance of restoring shalom to the home, neighborhood, and community. Restorative processes are built on the principle of identifying all the stakeholders and bringing them together to determine the most effective resolution to a conflict.

Identifying stakeholders on a large scale includes identifying all the significant individuals, groups, or agencies involved in a conflict. When an entire community is affected by injustice or oppression, the stakeholders should, therefore, include all individuals and systems on both sides of the conflict or influenced by it. When looking for stakeholders at the community level, leaders should ask who is missing from the table and what community-affecting systems, such as law enforcement, education, or health care, are outside the control of individual community members but should be engaged in the process or dialogue.

For most communities when a crime is committed, local law enforcement is called. The police then begin the process of determining what happens next. If an arrest is made, the judicial system determines the resolution. In this process the only person addressing the crime is the offender. Victims and other people impacted by the offender's actions tend to have a peripheral role, rarely having a voice in the outcome of the offender's crime. In restorative justice work, however, these people are considered stakeholders, and their voices are brought into the process.

When using these concepts outside a crime context, consider a situation that occurred in a small neighborhood where people didn't let their children play outside without supervision because of conflict. One mom said that her problem was not with the children interacting in an appropriate manner but rather with the parents' becoming involved in the children's squabbles. When this happened, the conflicts escalated into heated confrontations that led to neighbors keeping the children inside all day. This situation could benefit from a process that brings all the stakeholders (parents, children, and neighbors) into a dialogue. When all the stakeholders are present, they can learn how to resolve their conflicts in a healthy, appropriate manner.

Before inviting stakeholders to begin a dialogue, it is important to understand and implement other restorative justice and mediation concepts of accountability, positions vs. interests, creating a safe place, neutrality, and active listening. If the other components of restorative justice are not met, stakeholders should not begin dialogue. Though it is critical to identify all the stakeholders, it is disastrous to stop with that concept alone. In order to learn the language of shalom, we must learn and utilize all the components of restorative justice.

Elements of Mediation

Mediators are able to bring disputing parties together to discuss complex issues. In many cases, conflict can be resolved much more efficiently through mediation rather than through civil or criminal courts or other forms of dispute resolution. Thus, it is important to have a basic understanding of what makes the elements of mediation so effective. There are a variety of forms of mediation used in businesses, schools, families, civil cases, and even churches. These forms can be categorized as evaluative, facilitative, or transformative.

Some significant elements of mediation create opportunity for reconciliation:

Element 1: Balance of Power

In some forms of mediation, one role of the mediator is to create a balance of power in which both parties feel safe in addressing the conflict that brought them to the table. In restorative justice, creating a balance of power also creates a "safe place." The process of creating a balance of power and a safe place will be explained in more detail in Key 4.

Element 2: Neutrality

The concept of *neutrality* is one mediation tool. Mediators use neutral language in questioning, summarizing, restating, and reframing to allow participants to hear and identify the significant issues each person brings to the table. Neutrality will be addressed in detail in Key 5.

Element 3: Positions vs. Interests

A third element of mediation is understanding the difference between *positions* and *interests*. Positions are the circumstances that bring people to mediation. Interests are the personal values, emotions, and motives that drive people to the positions they take. The element of positions vs. interests is addressed in greater detail in Key 3.

Element 4: Solutions Generated by the Parties Themselves

The last component of mediation is the need for the parties involved to generate the solution themselves. After all, they are the ones who will leave the process and live with the results. Because the mediation participants must own the solutions, the mediator should not suggest possible solutions. He or she can, however, lead the parties through a reality check by asking questions to determine the effectiveness of the generated solutions. If the options are realistic, the parties involved will be significantly more likely to implement the solution.

Victim-offender mediation is a restorative justice form of mediation. VOM brings together victims of violent crimes and their offenders for purposes of insight and healing and can address highly complex needs and emotions. VOM processes allow the most extreme cases of opposing parties reflected in violent crimes to move toward healing and, at times, reconciliation. Since VOM processes work well in these incredibly difficult situations, it is reasonable to assume that they can also be used effectively in less complex situations outside the arena of criminal justice to address other forms of injustice.

Take It Further!

- Locate the Dispute Resolution Center near you.

- Find and sign up for mediation training.

- Read one book on restorative justice. Suggested titles include *Changing Lenses: A New Focus for Crime and Justice*, by Howard Zehr, or *The Little Book of Circle Processes: A New/Old Approach to Peacemaking*, by Kay Pranis. There are many possible choices. Just start reading.

the language of shalom.

2 Identify Differences Between Positions & Interests

The purposes of a person's heart are deep waters, but one who has insight draws them out.

—Proverbs 20:5 NIV

Effective mediation requires understanding the difference between positions and interests. *Positions* are the stands that people take when there is conflict or injustice. They are the demands or the bottom line of people on each side of a dispute. Typically, positions are non-negotiable. *Interests* are the personal values, emotions, and motives that drive people to the particular positions they take.

Trying to resolve conflict, facilitate reconciliation, or address injustice by focusing on a position will not be effective. Positions can be addressed, but the ongoing disputes between people will continue until the underlying interests are also addressed. The role of a mediator, then, is to actively listen to people and ask questions with the purpose of identifying their interests and moving them toward reconciliation. These underlying interests

19

become the building blocks of reconciliation. The following scenario demonstrates the difference between positions and interests.

Jane Smith is 72 years old and has lived in an older neighborhood for the past forty years. She has lived alone since her husband died three years ago. Carol Jones and her three sons live next door to Mrs. Smith. When the three boys were younger, they spent a great deal of time with Mrs. Smith and her husband, but now the boys are in their teens and are very active in school.

Recently the oldest boy got his driver's license. One morning as he was backing out to go to school, he accidently ran into Mrs. Smith's fence and destroyed her favorite flower garden. Carol told Mrs. Smith that she would have her son repair the fence and replace the garden, but Mrs. Smith refused to allow him to work in her yard and insisted Carol pay to have a professional make the repairs. Carol thought the request was unreasonable and only offered to make her son do the repairs. Mrs. Smith would not back down and took her concerns to the neighborhood association.

The association referred the matter to a local mediator. The mediation was scheduled, and in the beginning the women talked about the repairs and whether the request to hire a professional was reasonable. The mediator heard Mrs. Smith comment that the boys were never around much, so he asked, "Could you explain in a little more detail what you mean when you say the boys are never around?"

Her answer was that the boys used to spend a great deal of time with her and they were never around now. Through tears she said, "Maybe they just wanted to be around my husband, and now that he's gone they don't need me." Carol quickly responded that the boys still loved her and talked of her often, but their schedules had gotten so busy lately.

The mediator also noticed that Carol was very disturbed by the idea of hiring a professional and kept referring to how expensive that would be. The mediator asked Carol to explain her concerns about the costs. She explained that she had recently found out her husband had cancer, and they were facing large medical bills. As the two women heard each other's interests, the conversation shifted. Within an hour they had arrived at a viable solution for both.

In the beginning, the position of Mrs. Smith was that she wanted a professional to make her repairs. The position of Carol was that she did not want to hire a professional. But their interests were quite different. Mrs. Smith felt lonely and missed the boys from next door. She felt they had abandoned her since her husband died. Carol was worried about her husband's health and all the ramifications that held for her future.

Any agreement based solely on the position of whether or not to hire a professional would not have addressed the underlying interests of the neighbors. It might have been possible to "fix" that particular issue, but without addressing the underlying interests, the neighbors might have found themselves at odds with each other in the future.

Not only were the fence and garden repaired, but the relationship was repaired as well. The conflict arose from the circumstance, but in reality it was based on the interest of a broken relationship. The circumstance merely allowed the interest of that broken relationship to emerge and be addressed.

As mentioned earlier, it is important for people in mediation to generate the solution themselves. As reconcilers we should help people generate solutions based on their interests, not their positions. They know best how to address their personal interests, and they are the ones who will leave the mediation and have to live with the results.

Those working in community development ministries often help people with situations that are difficult to address and change. It is common to work diligently to address an issue, believe it to be resolved, and then learn shortly thereafter that the same issue has cropped up again. For instance, Christian community developers may help families with financial planning and budgeting. The family learns about budgeting, receives and creates a budget, and follows it for a period of time. The issue appears to be resolved. But sometimes, months later, the same family is in financial crisis again. It would be a mistake to sit down again and renew the commitment to the original budget or even create a new budget. Simply reinstituting the original solution would place all the emphasis on the position, which in this case is bad financial management. Instead, what must be determined are the interests in place that are causing the positions to occur.

Once the interests are identified, the solution can be built on those interests. It may be that a new budget is still needed, but there may be numerous other parts of the plan that need to be put in place as well. Some of the possible interests in this case may be fear or shame. If the family is operating out of fear, part of the plan could be to help them create an environment where they feel safe about their future. If the family feels shame, they may believe they deserve what they are getting, making it easy to stop following a budget. So a plan in that case should include working with the family to address the shame.

People's interests arise from their needs. Some basic human needs are safety, love, belonging, esteem, personal growth, fulfillment, responsibility, and stability. Psychologist Abraham Maslow developed a hierarchy of human needs that ranges from basic physiological needs to psychological and spiritual needs, each level of which must be satisfied before a person can successfully move to the next. For example, people whose basic need for food is not being met are unlikely to want to address interpersonal conflicts until they can quit worrying about going to bed hungry each night. If we are to be successful reconcilers, we must learn how to help people identify their specific interests (needs). Then we can move forward toward solutions.

Please note that it is not the job of development workers or mediators to decide the interests. It is their job to listen, ask the right questions, clarify answers, and help people articulate for themselves what values and motives are underlying the situation.

There are several ways to get past positions and move toward interests. The facilitator can try asking questions such as:

- Is this current situation satisfactory to you, or would you like to see something else?

- How do you feel about this particular situation?

- Are you saying that…?

- What do you need to make things better?

Once the facilitator thinks an interest has been identified, he or she should verify it with the person by saying something like, "It sounds to me like you are concerned about this because…" The person will either confirm or dismiss the statement. If confirmed, the facilitator has a foundation for beginning reconciliation. If dismissed, he or she should go back and ask more questions.

When working with people in conflict, identifying interests can be time-consuming. It would be much easier and quicker to take the position and start generating solutions right away. This approach, however, will be much more time-consuming in the long run because the situation will emerge again if interests are not addressed.

Learning how to listen for interests and ask appropriate questions takes thought and time. Try it, and see how you do. But most importantly, keep at it! Like learning any new language, it takes time and practice. But the reward is helping people find reconciliation that is true and lasting.

Take It Further!

Listen to people as they talk about injustice or problems and ask yourself:

- Do their comments reveal a position or an interest?

- What possible interests are motivating this person to take this position?

- What questions might be asked about this particular situation that can help identify position?

Practice & Expect Accountability

"This is the verdict: Light has come into the world, but people loved darkness instead of light because their deeds were evil. Everyone who does evil hates the light, and will not come into the light for fear that their deeds will be exposed."

—John 3:19-20 NIV

Another component of restorative justice processes, and victim-offender mediation in particular, is accountability. In VOM, responsibility and accountability by the offender are prerequisites in order to qualify for participation. If an offender does not take responsibility, then any face-to-face meeting with his or her victim has significant potential to create further harm. In cases of crime, the offender is the person who is incarcerated. But the term *offender* can be used for any person who does wrong or causes pain, annoys, or opposes.

Mediation processes build on the willingness of each person to take responsibility for his or her words and actions. Taking responsibility is not only a restorative justice mandate but also a biblical one. Reconciliation from a biblical perspective requires the prerequisite of accountability on the part of the offender. John 3:19-20 NIV says,

> "This is the verdict: Light has come into the world, but people loved darkness instead of light because their deeds were evil. Everyone who does evil hates the light, and will not come into the light for fear that their deeds will be exposed."

Notice the message of accountability in these words. People who love darkness and will not come into the light are not taking responsibility for their actions. According to scripture there is a need for acknowledgment and confession of sin. This sets in motion the process of reconciliation with a righteous and just God. In 1 John 1:9 NKJV, we read, "If we confess our sins, He is faithful and just to forgive us our sins and to cleanse us from all unrighteousness." According to this scripture, forgiveness—reconciliation with God—comes after confession of sins. If accountability and confession are necessary for reconciliation with God, it makes sense that they are also necessary in order to reconcile people to each other. While VOM does not base its accountability component on biblical demands, it does clearly recognize the human need to take full responsibility for actions and harms. Only then can reconciliation and healing take place. The language of shalom recognizes and bases accountability on biblical demands and speaks to those expectations when working with others.

Reconciliation between God and us begins when we acknowledge what we have done wrong. That is the first part of repentance, or turning away from sin. Reconciliation among individuals, families, and communities begins the same way. We must acknowledge our role in causing harm if we hope for reconciliation. We should strive for accountability and responsibility where harm has been done.

The Reconciler's Role

As reconcilers, it is not our role to determine who is guilty and who is innocent. This can be pretty touchy sometimes because trying to determine accountability can dissolve into judging others. When that happens, the reconciler has become a judge. It is human nature to do that. When listening to people's stories, it may become clear who is wrong and who is right. But we must allow the person to recognize his or her own wrongs. When we determine guilt, we are *placing* responsibility on someone instead of letting him or her *take* responsibility. "Sophie's Story" in Appendix B illustrates how to work with someone and allow him or her to personally take responsibility.

We can practice accountability in everyday situations. It is easy to see how other people do or do not take responsibility for the harms they have done. But we need to be intentional about acknowledging our own wrong acts, too. Being an effective minister of reconciliation is a lifestyle that requires us to be reconciled to people around us. It is hard to admit when we are wrong. But if we push past our own discomfort, admit our guilt, and take responsibility, this will help us grow in character. As we model speaking the language of personal accountability, we help create a safe environment. And when people feel safe, it is more likely that they will take responsibility.

When there has been tremendous harm done by one person to another, or one group to another, whoever created that harm must accept responsibility and admit guilt *before* beginning a process of reconciliation. In victim-offender mediation, the mediator determines accountability on the first visit. The degree of personal responsibility the offender demonstrates is used to determine if there should be a face-to-face meeting.

Absence of Accountability

The absence of accountability has great potential to allow continued harm. Violent offenders who refuse to take responsibility for their actions are very dangerous people. If they don't see anything wrong with their behavior, they feel there is no reason to change. A thief who sees nothing wrong with stealing will keep stealing. If a person hurts someone and feels justified in his or her actions, there is no reason for that person to change. When someone has been hurt and the offender refuses to take responsibility, there is potential for secondary harm or pain. The second source of pain comes from the offender's denial. The victim may ask questions such as, *Why won't he admit he is wrong? Why would she want to hurt me? Why is he still being so mean?*

If there is ongoing conflict or tension, it may be because the offender in the situation will not accept responsibility for harm. When others hurt us, our instinct is to put up an emotional wall to protect ourselves from future harm. If we burn a hand on a scalding skillet, we will use a pot holder next time. In the same way, when we have been hurt before, we try to find ways to protect ourselves from further emotional hurt.

Scripture speaks about taking accountability for past harms in Matthew 5:23-24 NIV. Jesus said,

> "Therefore, if you are offering your gift at the altar and there remember that your brother or sister has something against you, leave your gift there in front of the altar. First go and be reconciled to them; then come and offer your gift."

Notice that the responsibility for accountability is on the one at the altar who has done something wrong. The scripture refers to a specific event or act that occurred in the *past*. However, the act of reconciliation is a *now* process. The person must go *now* and address the harm that was done in the *past*.

Denial is different. Continuing to deny a harmful act from the past creates new harmful acts in the *present*. Denial is a second source of pain and can be more harmful than the original offense because it continues indefinitely. Just take a moment to think of a time when someone did or said something very hurtful to you and refused to take responsibility. Which was more painful—the initial hurt or the denial? What effect did denial have on your relationship with this person?

If you know one person has harmed another and yet denies any harm, facilitating a dialogue between them is not recommended. A dialogue without willingness on the part of the offender to accept personal responsibility can establish an imbalance of power. At this point the offender has the opportunity to re-harm the victim through denial.

Listening for Denial

One way to help people take appropriate responsibility for their actions without acting as a judge is by learning to speak the language of shalom. Learning to speak the language of shalom requires good listening skills. The reconciler should listen for ways that people avoid being accountable for their actions. Some ways to avoid responsibility include:

- Denial: *"I didn't do it."*

- Justifying: *"I had to do it because..."*

- Minimizing: *"What I did wasn't that big a deal."*

- Making excuses: *"It wasn't my fault because..."*

As reconcilers we must develop language skills to help people see their roles in situations. If the correct process is followed and the right questions are asked, we can help people own their roles in the conflict or situations. There are two approaches that can be used. After listening, we begin a dialogue that helps the excuse-maker recognize the lack of accountability and provides an opportunity for him or her to take responsibility. For example, this can be done by repeating back to the excuse-maker the words he or she used and follow with the question, *What do you think the other person would think upon hearing that?*

The second approach is to ask hard questions. Some examples of questions that can be asked to determine accountability are:

- *Can you tell me what you think your role in this situation is?*

- *How do you think the other person views you?*

- *What might cause him or her to view you that way?*

- *Do you have a role in how he or she views you?*

Even with our best language skills, there are times when people refuse to take responsibility for their actions. And when that happens we have to walk away from the reconciliation process, at least for a season.

Misplaced Responsibility

Sometimes a victim feels as if he or she has caused the offense. This is called misplaced responsibility. Have you ever heard someone who has experienced trauma or loss say something like, "This never would have happened if I hadn't ..." and then go on to describe what he or she did to cause the traumatic event? Listen carefully to determine if comments like this mean the individual is taking responsibility—or accepting misplaced responsibility. Sometimes people will take responsibility for the crimes of others. As ministers of reconciliation it is our job to help them recognize this and then encourage the real offender to take responsibility for the harm.

Disclaimers

There are several disclaimers, or extra conditions to consider, that should be mentioned about accountability. Just because a person does not take responsibility does not mean that some form of justice should not be pursued. If a person harms another and will not take responsibility, reconciliation is not likely to occur. But it may be necessary to take steps as a society to hold that person responsible for his or her actions. This is where the legal system should be utilized. Many thieves will not admit to stealing, but their personal acknowledgement is not the only criteria necessary for being held accountable.

Another disclaimer is that sometimes the lack of an admission of guilt or personal accountability does *not* prevent reconciliation. This happens in minor disputes between friends or between husbands and wives. There may be a conflict where each person feels the other is wrong, but neither will admit it. In these situations, the relationship is too important to allow the differences to be an ongoing issue, and they are put aside. Even though there is no confession on the part of either friend or partner, there is still some degree of taking responsibility for their actions. If people can acknowledge their differences in a way that each person agrees that the relationship is more significant than the differences, then the relationship can move forward in a healthy manner.

A reconciler uses skills to help people accept responsibility, but ultimately, being accountable is a choice that must be made by each individual. Personal accountability, like the personal choice to forgive, can't be demanded. We can force accountability to and with the laws of our land, but we cannot demand that someone take personal responsibility. Our role is to create an environment where the opportunity to be personally accountable for one's actions can become a reality.

Take It Further!

- Identify one time you were wrong, hurt someone, and did not take responsibility.

- Take responsibility for your harm. If possible, go to that person and attempt to repair the harm.

- Identify areas in your life or ministry where accountability is

the language of shalom

4 Create a Safe Place

not being required but should be.

The Lord also keeps safe those who suffer. He is a safe place in times of trouble.

—Psalm 9:9 NLV

Creating a safe place is foundational in reconciliation. It is possible to address dangerous issues while still feeling safe. This happens often in restorative justice processes such as victim-offender mediation. When a rape victim sits across from her rapist and discusses the trauma of the crime committed against her, safety must be addressed or she will never come to the table. Mediation recognizes the need to create a safe place to enable people to discuss topics and events that are unsafe.

Balance the Power

One method of creating a safe place is to create a balance of power where all involved know they will be heard. Skilled mediators are intentional about creating environments with a balance of power.

The fact that mediation consists of a structured process helps create a balance of power. Mediators learn to trust the process because although the actual problems being addressed in mediation can and do vary, the process itself does not vary. For this reason, the process can be applied to all facets of human interaction, conflict, communication building, and community development.

Although mediations are frequently done where one party does have power over another individual, the challenge is to balance that power without undermining the authority of one person or the other. If power is not balanced, one or both of the parties may fail to fully disclose the true interests at the heart of the problem. When people do not feel safe, they do not have an equal stake in the dialogue or outcome. In this situation they will not be fully engaged in addressing issues that need to be addressed to create a just and equitable result. Without that safety, people will address only positions, not interests.

The powerless may withhold critical information about their true interests to protect themselves from future abuse by the powerful. Without a balance of power, it is dangerous for the powerless to reveal interests because the powerful will then have the opportunity to use that vulnerability against them. When power is balanced, there is an opportunity for empowerment—not just in cases of rape but in any situation. And when David faces his Goliath, there is a tremendous sense of empowerment.

If a victim of violent crime can overcome fear enough to sit across the table from his or her offender, can you imagine the sense of empowerment that will carry over into other areas of life?

Structured Process

One factor that balances power in restorative justice processes is the structured process of mediation. It is critical that mediators learn to trust the process. As mentioned earlier, a structured dialogue can be used to address many issues. The process does not vary, but the actual disputes or problems will. Trusting the process is the life vest a mediator clings to when issues become difficult. Without a proven process, it is dangerous to bring a victim of violent crime face-to-face with the offender.

Victims tend to feel safe when they know the mediator is committed to the process and knows how to guide them through difficult dialogue. This is why it is important to follow up with ongoing training. In reconciliation work, people may trust us, as facilitators, with their deepest pain and shame. We must not take our responsibility lightly. "Karen's Story" in Appendix B is an account of an actual victim-offender mediation that illustrates the concept of creating a safe place.

When the concepts of balance of power and safe place are practiced in reconciliation, everyone involved can experience empowerment.

Take It Further!

- List processes that make you feel safe.

- During your next dialogue with two people, practice being equally engaged with both during the conversation.

the language of shalom.

5 **Be Neutral**

Let your conversation be always full of grace, seasoned with salt, so that you may know how to answer everyone.
—Colossians 4:6 NIV

Another mediation skill involves establishing the neutral role of the reconciler. Neutrality in its most basic form means to not take sides. It is essential for mediation because when the mediator doesn't take sides, the parties feel safe and recognize that they will have the opportunity to be heard. Neutrality is, therefore, a necessary skill for a reconciler, but it can be one of the most challenging and difficult mediation skills to develop.

To be successful, a reconciler must maintain a neutral position. There are several ways to maintain neutrality. One is to speak or ask questions equally to all those involved. This does not have to become robotic by asking the first party a question, waiting for an answer, and then asking the second party a question and waiting for an answer. Instead, the reconciler merely needs to ensure that one person is not being asked many questions while the other is asked only a few. If the focus is on one person more than the other, it doesn't take long for both parties to realize the process is not fair. Spending more time questioning one person over the other will cause the neglected person to feel left out. He or she will stop trusting the process and start building defensive walls. The neglected person may also become guarded or simply shut down the dialogue. At the very least, he or she may not reveal his or her true interest.

A facilitator in a community meeting can create defensiveness by not being attentive to the concept of neutrality. There will be dominant personalities as well as passive personalities in each community or neighborhood. A reconciler should listen to, ask, and speak to each person equally and not allow one person to dominate. This encourages less assertive people to participate in the conversation and creates a level playing field, a balance of power where everyone has input. When that happens, people feel safe. When everyone has input, people move past positions and reveal the interests linked to their values, emotions, and motives. If our personal opinions as reconcilers are so strong that maintaining neutrality isn't possible, we must remove ourselves and allow someone else to facilitate the process.

Reconcilers should also remain neutral about possible solutions. If we are not directly impacted by the issue being discussed, it isn't appropriate for us to come up with the solution. It might be tempting to look at a situation and say, "I know how to fix this problem. Just do A, B, C, and be done with it." But what seems right to us might not feel right to the people involved. In addition, if you offer a solution that does not work, the stakeholders will hold you responsible. This is why it is necessary to maintain neutrality and facilitate a process that allows people to determine their own solutions.

If people are allowed to discuss all the issues related to the problem and to spend sufficient time exploring options and testing those options, they are more likely to maintain the solution. This process can be effective in solving problems. If it is followed, stakeholders will recognize that they did the work. They will come away feeling empowered and more committed to the solutions.

Use Neutral Language

In the language of shalom, we use neutral communication processes to question, summarize, restate, and reframe. Doing so allows participants to identify significant issues that each person brings to the table. Of course using neutral language does not come naturally. It is an intentional, active skill that must be learned and practiced, just like mastering a foreign language. The language of shalom removes words or phrases that can indicate opinions and cause defensiveness in people. Neutral language also attempts to remove words that can elicit negative emotional reactions.

Sometimes we don't give much thought to the words we use. It is easy to say something that causes a negative reaction without intending to. Have you ever said something that hurt someone's feelings? Many times this happens, and we don't even remember the conversation. But the person we hurt remembers every word.

Our language is full of words that can be biased, potentially causing defensiveness and carrying negative messages. When working in community development, there are times that it is appropriate to use language that will stir up an emotional reaction. "Sophie's Story" in Appendix A is an example of the use of powerful language and neutral language. Neutral language should be the choice when seeking reconciliation. Powerful language should be used when trying to spur someone to action.

If we are trying to facilitate reconciliation where there has been injustice, neutral language is an effective tool. But it is important to remember that it is a tool, and we must carefully determine when it is appropriate to use that tool. There were times when Christ used powerful words, such as when He called the Pharisees a "brood of vipers" (see Matthew 12:34, 23:33; Luke 3:7).

But Christ also demonstrated the skill of neutrality. Look at the story of the woman at the well. Christ knew her sin but used neutral language when he talked to her. He asked her to go and get her husband. She replied, "'I have no husband.'" His response was, "'You are right when you say you have no husband. The fact is, you have had five husbands, and the man you now have is not your husband. What you have just said is quite true'" (John 4:17-18 NIV).

Jesus' response was a neutral way of saying, "Of course you do not have a husband because you are an adulteress." His choice of words allowed Him to confront the very real sin in her life by doing so in a way that maintained her dignity and left her open to continued dialogue. In response, the woman recognized the truth He spoke and went to tell others about Jesus. Here was a man who had just confronted her sin. She not only wanted to be around Him, but she went and found others to bring to Him as well. This is a beautiful example of how powerful neutral language can be.

Christ interacted with the woman. He knew she was a sinner, but He was more concerned about her redemption. He saw the sin, but He also saw her potential and chose words that spoke to that. He provided the opportunity for reconciliation. Not only was the woman changed, but so was her community.

The skill of neutrality takes the mediation process to the place where reconciliation can happen. What Christ has done for us highlights the difference between the basic mediation communication tool of neutrality and the fuller language of shalom. Neutrality paves the way for repentance, redemption, unity, and reconciliation, but the language of shalom speaks to potential.

Suspend Judgment

We are all quick to judge. We all have opinions. It is human nature to evaluate and then formulate opinions. In every situation there will be differences of opinion and perspective. In the reconciliation process, each of us—even the facilitator—will have an opinion about a situation. But neutrality requires that we ***temporarily*** suspend judgment of those in the process of reconciliation. As reconcilers listen to people tell their stories, they experience normal human emotions. These emotions may lead to favoring one person over another, believing that one is more truthful than the other or that the motives of one person are more valid than those of the other. The challenge is to identify personal bias and suspend judgment to keep that bias out of the process.

Christ is the ultimate example of suspended judgment. He walked among us and hung out with sinners. He preserved our dignity and entered into a relationship with us. He loved us. He experienced our humanness and suspended judgment of our sins in order to save us. In this state of suspended judgment, we can choose to be in relationship with Him. It is no mistake that Christ is called a mediator (1 Timothy 2:5; Hebrews 8:6, 9:15, 12:24). He took our sins on Himself and allowed us to enter into relationship with Him; we have the opportunity to take responsibility for our sin, repent, and enter into relationship with Him as our Redeemer. That relationship alone reconciles us to God. This same process can be used as the model for helping people reconcile with each other.

Many times we don't want to suspend judgment because we feel we know what is right and what is wrong. We want bad people to be punished and understand that there are negative consequences of sin. While it is necessary for our society to have laws and a judicial system to maintain order, as reconcilers God calls us to something greater. He asks us to be willing to temporarily suspend judgment in order to enter into dialogue with each other.

Bear in mind, judgment is only suspended temporarily and accountability must still be present. Our status as sinners before God does not change in that moment of temporarily suspended judgment. During that time God offers us reconciliation through faith in his son, Jesus. A final judgment will still occur based on the decision we made during that time of suspended judgment. And since Christ is our example in all things, it is logical to follow His method of reconciling us to Himself.

The process in itself facilitates neutrality. As neutrality is modeled, people will begin to operate in a similar manner. As the facilitator maintains neutrality and focuses on the process, the reconciling parties are forced to do so as well. The process may begin with identifying facts and feelings associated with the issue. Neutral questions are asked, comments are used to clarify, and dialogue continues. The very nature of the process forces the participants to partially suspend judgment through something as simple as taking turns in providing information and answering questions. Taking turns creates, or forces, suspended judgment, if only for a brief moment while one person waits for the other person to finish speaking. It is often in the time of suspended judgment that interests and common ground are identified and, in many cases, people begin to view each other differently. If facilitated correctly, the parties can begin to see the humanness of the "enemy." That realization of each other's humanness, dignity, and interests can dramatically change predetermined positions, judgments, and solutions the people had before coming into the process.

Take It Further!

- Over the next week, listen and write down five comments people make that are negative and cause defensiveness.

- Try to rewrite those comments in a way that is not negative but still keeps the message the same.

the language of shalom. 6 **Practice Active Listening**

Carry each other's burdens, and in this way you will fulfill the law of Christ.

—Galatians 6:2 NIV

Any basic communication course provides instruction in the important concept of active listening. Developing good listening skills is also a vital part of becoming an effective reconciler. Before we can help people reconcile, the first step is to listen to their stories. There are times we must not ask questions but simply listen, and we must listen before we can understand the situation.

Typically we listen for one or two purposes. Sometimes we listen with the sole purpose of learning, as happens in classrooms or during Bible study or teaching situations. We can simply listen to a person's story or background to learn more about him or her. We can also listen with the goal of hearing the heart of the speaker. There are tender moments when we find ourselves in a place where people trust us with their deepest pain or shame.

When this happens, we must recognize the sacred privilege we are being offered as we hold their story—that is, we carry the burden of their story or their pain. In these situations our goal is to allow the person to be heard.

Listening in the language of shalom involves learning and letting others be heard. We listen to learn the facts of the situation. We listen in order to hold the story of the suffering. We also listen to gain insight. A reconciler must patiently listen to the whole story. Then he or she can begin to ask questions that will help people move past pain and/or shame. When we listen with this goal, we can begin to fulfill the scripture that calls us to "bear one another's burdens."

In biblical days, bearing someone's burden meant the physical act of carrying something for an individual. For purposes of reconciliation, we can think of it as taking up the pain, struggles, or shame that someone is experiencing. Galatians 6:2 NIV says, "Carry each other's burdens." This language implies the act of holding. When we listen to others, we should strive to "hold" their story. But be aware that holding the burdens of others can lead to strong emotions. It is important to not allow fear to keep us from reaching out and touching others. Galatians 6:2 also implies that bearing the burdens of the one who is hurting means going some distance with him or her. Some burdens are heavy and some stories are difficult to hold, but we must be willing. Bearing the burdens of others is so vital that the verse goes on to say that in doing so, we "fulfill the law of Christ." The language of shalom helps us bear one another's burdens through active listening.

Active Listening Skills

There are some basic skills we can refine to become more effective listeners. These include facial expressions, gestures, eye contact, posture, questioning, and restating. Our expressions show whether or not we are truly listening to someone. If the story is funny, we smile. If the story is sad, our eyes may fill with tears. People can tell by our faces if we are following the story or thinking about something else. Our posture also sends a message. Sitting in a position that faces the speaker indicates that we are open to the story. Leaning toward the speaker from time to time indicates that we are engaged in what is being said.

If we tell people we want to hear what they have to say but our facial expressions are disconnected from the story, the speaker may shut down. This is because people believe what they see rather than what they hear. If we ask someone "How are you today?" and the answer "I am fine" is given with slumped shoulders and downcast eyes, do we believe what he or she said—or what we saw? People we are communicating with watch us the same way. If we say we are listening but our body language and facial expressions indicate we have checked out, the speaker may not want to share his or her story. Even if he or she does share, we will probably get the "nutshell" version. Without knowing the full story with all the details, there will be only a small chance of hearing the interests below the positions.

Asking questions indicates active listening. There are times when the listener may need clarification and should ask a question. That question indicates that the listener is engaged in the story. The same is true for restating. To restate, a listener might say something like, "So you are saying that…"

Eye contact is another active listening skill. In the culture of the United States and other westernized countries, looking someone in the eye while he or she is speaking is a sign that we are listening. However, in some cultures, direct eye contact is considered rude. If the people involved in your dialogue are from a different culture, it is a good idea to research their cultural preferences with regard to eye contact. If it is appropriate to give eye contact, then the listener should. There are some times, however, when a speaker begins to share deeply painful or shameful details of a story. If he or she looks away, we should look away, too. This is a sign of respect. The goal of active listening, no matter the situation, is to allow others to know we are present in their stories and their lives.

Take It Further!

- Read a book or take a course in basic communication and active listening.
- Practice active listening by using these skills with a friend or family member.

the language of shalom.

7 Identify Effective Local Reconciliation Ministries

As iron sharpens iron, so one person sharpens another.
—Proverbs 27:17 NIV

This chapter is not complicated or long. In fact it is short and to the point.

Find other reconciliation facilitators in your area. Too often ministries operate in a vacuum. Leaders may know the value of working collaboratively yet often find that the time to build those relationships is scarce. Limited time, however, should not prevent leaders, and those seeking to facilitate reconciliation, from learning and improving. In the beginning, "The Lord God said, 'It is not good for man to be alone'" (Genesis 2:18a NIV). God knew we needed each other. He created us to need and learn from each other. The task is finding those who can provide greater insight.

Often when we look to others for insight, we limit the search to groups who appear to be like-minded and are doing the same type of work we do. While this can be effective, the search should not stop there. Be willing to search outside your normal circle of influence. To learn to become a more effective reconciler, seek out mediators, counselors, restorative justice programs, and practitioners. Find out if there is a Dispute Resolution Center in your area. Do online searches to explore outside your area for resources that may be lacking. But most importantly, seek.

Take It Further!

- Go.

- Find.

- Learn.

con.clusion.

Words are important to God. When He created this world, He could have done it by any method. But He chose words.

> Then God **said**, "Let there be light"... Then God **said**, "Let there be an open space between the waters. Let it divide waters from waters"... Then God **said**, "Let the waters under the heavens be gathered into one place. Let the dry land be seen"... Then God **said**, "Let plants grow .... Let fruit trees grow...."
> —Genesis 1:3, 6, 9, 11 NLV

The Bible is full of references to the value of spoken words. Just a few of these are:

> The LORD was with Samuel as he grew up, and he let none of Samuel's **words** fall to the ground.
> —1 Samuel 3:19 NIV

> The centurion replied, "Lord, I do not deserve to have you come under my roof. But just say **the word**, and my servant will be healed."
> —Matthew 8:8 NIV

> They triumphed over him by the blood of the Lamb and by **the word** of their testimony...
> —Revelation 12:11 NIV

Our scripture is the *Word of God*. In Psalm 141:3 NIV, David asked God to set a guard over his mouth and keep watch over the door of his lips. Proverbs 13:3 NIV says that those who guard their words will preserve their lives. If God recognizes the value of the spoken word, we should as well.

I pray that you will learn the language of shalom so that your words can help you bring reconciliation to your family, your community, and our world.

appendix a

Karen's Story

An Illustration of Creating a Safe Place and Balancing Power

S he climbed out of the back seat, keeping her eyes fixed on the asphalt of the parking lot. The mantra in her mind was simply, "Breathe, Karen. Breathe."

The journey that had led up to this day had begun four months earlier when she met David. David was the mediator assigned to her case to prepare her for the face-to-face meeting with her offender. It had been ten years since the original crime and its associated trauma. The initial trauma had faded, but the fear and pain and yearning for answers had not. In fact, the searching for answers had increased. There was so much she didn't understand about what had happened, so much that didn't make sense because there simply were not enough details to complete the story. Tragically, the person who knew the rest of the story was the very person who had stormed in and ripped her life into pieces ten years before. The ragged bits of that story had blown away with the raging wind of his crime.

She and David had met several times during the past four months to get to know one another and ensure that this process would be safe. David had explained that the victim-offender mediation process was created to help victims of violent crime heal. He was kind yet firm and helped her understand what to expect.

As part of the process, Karen wrote down a lot of questions and things she wanted to say to Thomas, her offender. The night before the meeting, as she reread her questions, Karen became overwhelmed with fear. She called several friends and asked them to pray, telling them, "If a person can die of fear, I might die tomorrow." As Karen stepped out of the car, she felt as if those prayers were propelling her toward the mediation room.

It was hard to believe that the small table where David sat was going to be the only barrier between her and Thomas. Karen took her seat to the left of David, her body trembling uncontrollably. Thomas entered and sat directly across from her on David's right. She had to swallow between each shallow breath.

Karen's mind raced. *What am I doing here? Why did I think this was a good idea?* As she questioned her decision to be in this room, David began to speak. His words calmed her, and his voice snapped her out of her rambling thoughts. His gaze was soft, but he was confident. She thought back over the past four months of working with David. She trusted him. Even though they had known each other for only a short time, she felt that he was deeply committed to her in this process. David made her feel safe. It was an odd combination. She felt safe when she looked at David, but when she glanced at Thomas, fear bubbled up inside her. She decided to try to move forward.

Karen and Thomas spoke for hours. Tears flowed, voices cracked and rose in tone, and answers were found. As they talked, Karen realized that her fear was gone. She was still sitting across from the man who had torn apart her life, but now the fear was gone. David had created this opportunity. He knew that she had it in her to face her monsters, and he had willingly joined her for the battle.

Karen realized she didn't have to hate or fear Thomas any longer. He was only a man—a man who could no longer touch her, a man who was more broken than she was. Knowing this helped Karen realize that Thomas no longer had any power over her. He would not stalk her and terrify her in her dreams anymore. He was just a broken man she couldn't hate. Karen knew Thomas needed to hear that he was forgiven. She surprised herself when she said, "Thomas, I want you to know I forgive you for what you did." Across the table Thomas wept like a child.

As the meeting ended, Karen felt a power she had never felt before. She had faced her monsters and won! The walk from the meeting room back to the car seemed to be a completely different path. She knew this was the way she had entered a few short hours ago, but everything looked different. She knew her life would never be the same. Yes, there would still be tattered places in her heart, but there were no more gaping holes. On the way home, she realized David had given her an amazing gift. David had made it safe to sit in the den of a monster and not die. She would always be thankful to him, but he did not need her gratitude. He was her mediator. He had done what he had said he would do. And it had worked.

$$\sim$$

The story of Karen and Thomas is the story of the victim-offender mediation of a violent crime. The VOM process was created to address crime but should not be limited to that arena. Read the story of Sophie in Appendix B to see that these processes can and are being used to bring the same type of impact to the work of Christian community development.

appendix b

Sophie's Story
An Example of Restorative Justice Concepts Applied
to Christian Community Development

*C*ompassionate confrontation was the term Dave Clark used to describe the style I use with the women who live at Perpetual Help Home where I am the director. Dave is with Christian Community Development Association, and he coined the phrase when he toured the facility in 2012. Part of his tour involved hearing the dramatic stories of three women who live at Perpetual Help Home, a Christian community development ministry. These three women also run the Center for Peace, a non-traditional business similar to a social enterprise. The Center is operated using innovative and non-traditional business methods. It also manages numerous ministries in which the women volunteer helping victims, criminal justice professionals, families of victims and offenders, and those still in addiction and prostitution. Sophie was one of the three women who shared her story.

When the youngest of Sophie's sons was 14 years old, she got a divorce. In her depression, she turned to crack cocaine. Her addiction was instant, and she began a dark journey that ended in a very public arrest. With frustration verging on anger she gushed, "I just wish people would look past my mistake and see that I am human."

As she tried to continue her story, I interrupted and said, "It was a crime, not a mistake." Sophie acknowledged that she had committed a crime that had sent her to prison. What she meant was that her mistake was when she started using drugs. I repeated, "It was not a mistake. It was a crime. The purchase of crack is a crime." I felt it was important that Sophie understood the fact that she was minimizing her behavior—behavior that had caused her to plummet into addiction, prison, and poverty. Realizing the truth, she nodded. It was an awkward and blunt conversation, but part of my job is to bring up tough subjects. Sophie knew that I loved her and was deeply invested in her recovery.

When Sophie finished, Dave said, "For most people reconciliation is an option, but here at Perpetual Help Home, reconciliation is a mandate! You are also not afraid to use compassionate confrontation to help people see the truth."

The meeting ended, but I kept turning the words *mandated reconciliation* and *compassionate confrontation* over in my mind. Was this really a good way to describe what we do? I intentionally weave the concepts of restorative justice into the fabric and personality of Perpetual Help Home. Infusing restorative justice principles into everything we do has increased and sped up reconciliation and transformation in our women's lives. The women of Perpetual Help Home know restorative justice is the heart of our ministry. Restorative justice puts a face on crime. Personal accountability to repair the harm they caused is the first step in the process. Practical actions are necessary to address those harmed by their behaviors.

For some reason, I could not get past the comments Sophie had made about her "mistake." By minimizing and justifying her actions, she was showing a lack of accountability. Sophie was not just a homeless woman in poverty. She had played a role in her situation. Restorative justice processes promote personal accountability. Without personal accountability for harm, reconciliation is very difficult to achieve. After mulling it over, I decided that accountability and reconciliation *are* mandates at Perpetual Help Home.

The next day, I pulled Sophie aside to address her excuses. Sophie seethed with anger. Her greatest sorrow was that her behaviors had estranged her from her sons. She was adamant that I understand how devastating this was for her. I acknowledged her pain, but pain did not erase the need to take responsibility for what she had done. Still Sophie continued to minimize her role. Finally I said, "Sophie, I just wonder if God is not allowing you to reconcile with your sons in order to protect them from your excuses!"

Sophie was enraged as she said, "I can admit the truth to you and other addicts but not to…."

"…to the people you hurt?" I asked.

Sophie began to cry.

Standing in the warm sun, I gave Sophie a hug. Again I told her I really felt that God might be blocking an attempt at reconciliation until she was willing to take full responsibility for her actions. She had to be accountable to the people she had hurt. "Just think of one or two people in your hometown whom you can go to and make things right," I said.

Immediately Sophie said, "I know where to start. I took money from a man who owned a local store. I knew he was struggling." In her addiction, it was easy to ignore his needs. But now it was not. She dropped her eyes and said, "I am so ashamed."

"Is it time for you to go back and talk to that man?" I asked. Sophie began to tremble. It was one thing to talk about it, but another thing to do it. "Sophie, are you ready to make things right?"

That night I questioned my stern words to Sophie. I thought about the term *compassionate confrontation*. Had I pushed her too hard? Sophie's angry reaction made me second-guess my methods.

The next morning I asked Sophie what she had decided. "I just need to go," she replied. Then she began to tremble again.

"Sophie, it was for the joy set before Him that Christ endured the cross. He saw past the shame and pain of His death to the people He would save in the future. Maybe you were the joy he saw." If Sophie could face her fears and shame, she might see joy on the other side of her pain.

The trip was set for the next afternoon. Sophie had hoped to wait until the following week, but it was not an option if I was to go along. Sophie decided to take $500 from her savings to give to the store owner. This was a personal decision. Five hundred dollars was almost a third of the money she had worked hard to save for the last ten months. It was also the exact amount of the hot check she had written to him years before.

We talked as we drove. Because of my background as a restorative justice mediator, I thought it would be a good idea if we role-played some different scenarios as we drove. "What will you do if he gets angry?" I asked. "What will you do if he tells you to leave or refuses to take the money?"

Sophie laughed, "There is no way that will happen! He will take the money." During the drive she also talked about her four sons. Three were successful professionals, and the youngest was in college. She had contact with two of them, but the other two would have nothing to do with her. She hadn't spoken to them in years. Someone in her family had told her that her oldest, Joseph, hated her. She was ashamed.

We drove past places familiar to Sophie, places she had worked, her former house, and her ex-husband's home. She hadn't expected anyone to be home at that last location, but his car was there and someone was on the porch. We drove on to complete the task at hand.

When we arrived at the store, there were no customers and the owner was outside. Sophie noticeably trembled, as she had done almost constantly since the beginning of the compassionate confrontation. Sophie swung open the car door and got out. "Do you remember me?" she asked.

The man squinted up into her face for a long time. Finally he said slowly, "Yes, I believe I do."

"I want to pay you back for the hot check I wrote you when I was doing drugs before I went to prison."

"Didn't you make restitution?"

"No. I was ordered to, but I never paid any money. I just sat it out in jail."

The man looked into Sophie's eyes but wouldn't accept the money. Remembering our rehearsal in the car, Sophie continued to insist.

"How about you put it in God's offering plate?" he asked.

"Will you make it an offering at your church?" Sophie suggested.

"Well, I guess I could do that," he admitted. After Sophie handed the money to him, they began talking about old times, neighbors, and family members. Sophie looked pleased when he told her how good she looked. Finally he asked, "Why are you doing this? You served your time."

"It's just right. It has been a burden for so long. I had to do it."

As we drove away, Sophie's trembling changed to giggling. She giggled like a schoolgirl. Sophie had faced her shame, and the reward was kindness from the one she had harmed. We were both so relieved. Sophie's joy was proof that compassionate confrontation was the right thing to do after all.

As we were heading out of town, I had an idea. "Let's drive by your ex-husband's house again!" Sophie wasn't sure about that, but for some reason I had an urge to go back. She finally agreed.

When we arrived, the person we had seen earlier was still on the porch. Sophie whispered, "It's Joseph, my son! I have to stop!" As she got out of the car, he glanced up. "Hi, Joseph," she said.

Unsure at first, he finally recognized her and said, "Hi, Mom." Then he smiled.

"I could really use a hug, Joseph." He raised arms, which were covered in car grease, to show his mother why he couldn't hug her. He had been working on his car, but Sophie walked right into those open greasy arms. "How are your brothers?" she asked.

"Thomas is in the house," said Joseph. Thomas came out with a bewildered look on his face. Sophie opened her arms to him, and he hugged her. Both of the sons Sophie had not spoken to in years were standing on the porch talking to her and smiling.

Thomas smiled and said, "I love you, Mom, but I am just not sure what to say." *Awkward* was the best word to describe the conversation. Sophie understood and graciously retreated. "I love you both," she stated.

Both young men replied, "We love you, too."

The moment Sophie heard those words, her world changed. All the way home she and I marveled at the miracle of reconciliation that had happened. Sophie had yearned for the love of her boys, and today she had heard the words, "I love you, Mom."

The goal of the trip had not been reconciliation with her sons. It had been about personal accountability and making things right with someone else she had harmed. She had gone home to voluntarily make restitution for a crime she had committed years ago, a debt that the State of Texas considered paid. Obedience had led Sophie back to the scene of her crime, and the reward had been phenomenal. The shame was gone. The sorrow of losing her sons' love was gone. Joseph and Thomas were the two sons who had hated her and not spoken to her, but on this day they had smiled at their mother, hugged her, and told her they loved her.

How had God pulled this off? Though these two sons did not live in that town, they had just happened to be in town on the same day! We thought my schedule had dictated the day, but now we knew it had been God!

We were so amazed that all we could say for the next ten minutes were things like, "Wow!" and "That was so freaking amazing!" We recognized that we had just been standing on holy ground. God had allowed me to be present as He demonstrated the gospel to Sophie and her sons by working a miracle of reconciliation for them.

Do principles of restorative justice and Christian community development need to be intertwined? Sophie and I think they do. Is compassionate confrontation a good thing? On Sophie's day it was. Can reconciliation be mandated in ministry? Ask Sophie.

As we giggled and cried on the way home, I asked Sophie where she was on the shame meter. "Yesterday's shame is today's glory," she replied.

"Amen, sister! Amen!"

about the author

Cheryl Miller lives in Victoria, Texas, with her husband, Leslie. She is the mother of four adult children and the grandmother of four. She has been the executive director of Perpetual Help Home since 1999. Through her leader-ship the program has grown to become the largest housing program for women in her community, with over 1,200 women

©2012 by Kevin Jordan

and children having passed through the doors of Perpetual Help Home in the past thirteen years.

Cheryl has volunteered as a mediator for the Victim-Of-fender Mediation Dialogue program since 2001. She has logged over 1,000 hours of mediation experience working with victims of violent crimes and their offenders. Her training in mediation includes forty hours of basic mediation training, thirty hours of family mediation training, forty hours of training in the Victim-Offender Reconciliation Program at Fresno Pacific University, and ninety-six hours of Victim-Offender Mediation/Dialogue training with the Texas Department of Criminal Justice. She is a Credentialed Advanced Mediator through the Texas Mediator Credentialing Association.

perpetual help home and center for peace

Perpetual Help Home is a permanent supportive housing program that works with women and children. It is a faith-based program that gives women and their children the opportunity to make changes in life. While the home is fairly structured, it is built on the concept of empowering women to take control of their lives.

At Perpetual Help Home, women are required to work or attend school full-time, attend church and Bible study, and take part in some form of twelve-step program. In the beginning phases of their stay, all the women's income is managed by staff in a resident fund account. There is a strict budget that each woman must follow: 10 percent of all funds is tithed to the church she attends, 15 percent is paid as rent to the home, 25 percent can be spent for personal expenses, and 50 percent must be kept in that account as her savings.

The program operates on a system of levels where women

slowly transition from dependence on the organization to independence. Each level allows for greater autonomy and greater responsibility. Before women leave the home, they manage all their own finances and decisions.

The Center for Peace is the social enterprise that is run by the women who live in Perpetual Help Home. The Center was created to provide on-the-job training for residents of the home. The Center earns revenue through providing training in multiple areas and offering training to churches. Wholistic Community Development training educates churches on effective community ministry methods, and Addict411 trains churches to effectively minister to addicted individuals.

The Center also trains women in the community with a program called Tools for Success, created by women on staff at the Center. This unique training allows women to teach other women the skills they themselves have learned. The training addresses empowerment by teaching entrepreneurship, work ethics, self-esteem, computer skills, and skills for working in a professional setting. This training has been so successful that it is an essential part of life at Perpetual Help Home, and all newer residents are trained by established residents through Tools for Success.

The Center for Peace also houses all the restorative justice ministries of Perpetual Help Home. The women who live at the home are required to give back to the community by working in one of the restorative justice ministries. Each component is designed to address a different group impacted by crime, such as victims, families, offenders, and criminal justice professionals. Among the programs offered are Crime Victim Support Group, Night to Light (a prostitute outreach ministry), Letters from Home (writing to women still incarcerated), Criminal Justice Professional "Thanks" (showing gratitude to people involved in our local criminal justice system), and Making It Right (assisting victims who have been impacted by theft). All these ministries are designed to focus on the human element of crime and have had tremendous impact on Perpetual Help Home residents.

suggested resources

Bazemore, Gordon, and Mara Schiff. *Restorative Community Justice: Repairing Harm and Transforming Communities*. Cincinnati: Anderson Publishing, 2001.

MacRae, Allan, and Howard Zehr. *Little Book of Family Group Conferences: New Zealand Style*. Intercourse, PA: Good Books, 2004.

Pranis, Kay. *Little Book of Circle Processes: A New/Old Approach to Peacemaking*. Intercourse, PA: Good Books, 2005.

Restorative Justice: A Framework for Fresno. February 2001. Web. 29 June 2012.

Umbreit, Mark S. *The Handbook of Victim Offender Mediation: An Essential Guide to Practice and Research*. Edison, NJ: Jossey-Bass, 2000.

Umbreit, Mark S. *Mediating Interpersonal Conflicts: A Pathway to Peace*. Eugene, OR: Wipf and Stock Publishers, 2006.

Zehr, Howard. *Changing Lenses: A New Focus for Crime and Justice*. Harrisonburg, VA: Herald Press, 2005.

Zehr, Howard. *Little Book of Restorative Justice*. Intercourse, PA: Good Books, 2002.

CPSIA information can be obtained at www.ICGtesting.com
Printed in the USA
LVOW012332040912

297379LV00001B/2/P